Contents

Any words appearing in the text in bold, **like this,** are explained in the glossary. You can also look out for them in the "Wet Words" box at the bottom of each page.

Twister!

It is a quiet summer afternoon. It is warm and sunny, but slowly the sunshine fades. Tall, threatening clouds grow high into the sky. Now it is dark as night. Lightning flashes around the sky. **Torrential** rain pours down. **Hail** the size of golf balls crashes to the ground. A spinning **funnel** of air drops from the clouds. It reaches down and touches the ground. A **twister** is on the way.

> " It was like a big vacuum cleaner that sucked everything up. "
>
> Mike Cox, Texas Department of Safety, Jarrell, Texas, 1997

This tornado (twister) is black with dust. ▷

debris   bits and pieces of wrecked houses, cars, and other objects
random   happens without any pattern or choice

Deadly winds

The tornado quickly turns black as the funnel sucks up tons of dust. It gets closer and closer. Then comes a deafening rumble like a giant train rushing past. The strongest winds in the world have arrived. The whirling monster rips houses to shreds. It throws cars high into the air. Flying **debris** is everywhere. It is **chaos.**

The tornado disappears as quickly as it arrived. It leaves behind a trail of complete **destruction.**

Random killers

Tornadoes are the most violent and intense storms on Earth. They can grow to more than half a mile across. Inside are winds blowing at about 300 miles (500 kilometers) per hour. The tornado's winds suck in and destroy anything in its path. Tornadoes move **randomly** across the landscape. **Victims** often have little warning. Every year in the United States, tornadoes kill about 80 people.

Where is it dangerous to take shelter from a tornado?

Which type of clouds might bring a tornado?

What is a waterspout?

torrential   like a torrent, which is a rushing stream of liquid
twister   common name for a tornado

Tornado Science

A tornado is a column of air that spins at incredible speeds. Tornadoes only happen underneath huge thunderstorms. They come out from the bottom of thunderclouds. Heavy rain, **hail**, and lightning are always close by when tornadoes happen.

Supercells

Only monster thunderstorms are powerful enough to make tornadoes. They grow where huge blocks of warm and cold air meet. These huge thunderstorms are called **supercells**. They can last for many hours.

Making clouds

A cloud is made up of millions of tiny drops of water or tiny bits of ice. Clouds form when warm, moist air cools down. This happens when warm air moves upward through colder air.

The air is moist because it contains **water vapor.** Cooling makes the water vapor **condense** to form tiny water droplets. The same thing happens when you breathe onto a cold mirror.

This storm was over Florida. Blocks of cold and warm air met and there were **severe** thunderstorms. These created many tornadoes.

▽

Stormy Words   condense   when a gas turns into a liquid
cumulonimbus   very tall, large cloud

Thunderclouds

Thunderclouds are the biggest clouds of all. Weather experts call them **cumulonimbus** clouds. They form when warm, moist air rises up in a fast **current** called an **updraft.** As the air cools, the invisible water vapor condenses to form the water droplets you can see. These make up huge clouds.

The updraft only stops when it reaches about 32,800 ft (10,000 m) above Earth's surface. Here, the air spreads out, giving the cloud a shape like a hammer. This is called an anvil top.

△ This is a big thunderstorm. You can see the anvil top, where the cloud has spread out.

Warm, moist air rises quickly. As it rises, the air cools and clouds are formed. ▽

Breaking through

The updrafts in a supercell thunderstorm are incredibly strong. Sometimes they are strong enough to make a bulge in the top of a thundercloud. A bulging top is a good way to recognize a supercell.

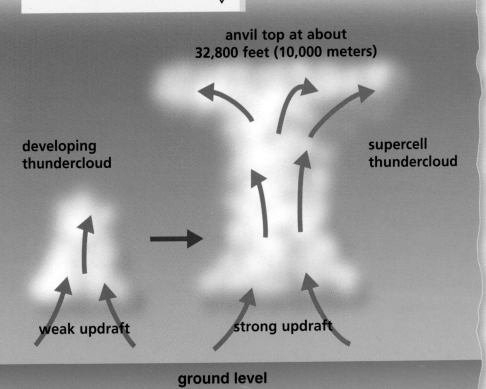

anvil top at about
32,800 feet (10,000 meters)

developing
thundercloud

supercell
thundercloud

weak updraft

strong updraft

ground level

updraft   current of air that flows upward
water vapor   water in the form of an invisible gas

A spinning storm

Sometimes the air inside a thunderstorm begins to spin. It forms a turning **funnel** of air called a **vortex**. A tornado happens when the bottom of a vortex touches the ground.

Now you see it

Water droplets can make the vortex look white or gray. The tornado sucks dust from the ground. The bottom of the tornado turns the same color as the dust. Sometimes tornadoes are invisible, until they begin to suck up dust.

A long, thin tornado vortex snakes down to the ground. The tornado's base is dark because of dust.

atmosphere   layer of air around Earth
funnel   shape that is like a cone with a long, thin section at the bottom

Tornado shapes and sizes

Some tornadoes look shapeless, like a cloud of dust. Others are very wide. They look like an upside-down bell. Some look like an elephant's trunk. Others are very thin, like a snake. Most tornadoes change shape at some point.

A funnel cloud is △ reaching down from the base of a thundercloud over Kansas.

Wide and narrow

Tornadoes come in a wide range of sizes. The average tornado is about 490 ft (150 m) wide where it touches the ground. Tornadoes can be as small as 164 ft (50 m) across. Giant tornadoes grow to 1 mi (1.6 km) across.

Spinning air

At different heights in the **atmosphere**, winds can blow in different directions. If this happens in a thunderstorm, it makes the air inside start to spin. The turning air is pulled into the **updraft**. This creates a huge, spinning column of rising air inside the thunderstorm.

Sometimes the bottom end of the spinning column of air dips down, beneath the base of its thundercloud. It sucks up more warm air from under the cloud. This makes it spin even faster, making a vortex. When the vortex touches the ground, it becomes a tornado.

vortex scientific name for a spinning column of air

Inside a tornado

You have seen what a tornado looks like from a distance, but what would one look like close up? What happens inside? The answers are hard to find. People who are hit by tornadoes are normally hiding in shelters and do not see anything. It is almost impossible and very dangerous to go inside a tornado with a camera.

This is what we know about tornadoes already. The air around the bottom of a tornado is sucked into the **vortex** at great speed. Then, it spirals upward into the cloud above. The air drags in dust and **debris**. Heavy bits of debris are thrown out sideways as they rise.

◁ Just a few hours of intense rain from **severe** thunderstorms caused this flash flooding in southwest France in 1992.

Tornado weather

Bad weather always comes with tornadoes. The thunderstorms create intense lightning, giant **hail** stones, and heavy rain. This often causes **flash floods.** Flash floods can cause lots of damage, too.

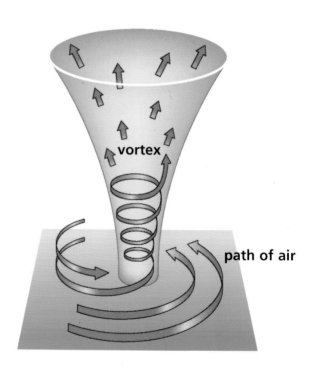

vortex

path of air

Inside a tornado, the air swirls ▷ around and upward. It forms a vortex. The air lifts up objects as large as cars and animals.

evidence proof that something has happened
eyewitness   person who saw something happen

View from inside

In the center of a tornado vortex, the air may be clear and move at much lower speeds. **Evidence** for this comes from an **eyewitness** story. In 1943 a farmer named Roy Hall became one of the few people to see inside a tornado and survive. As the tornado destroyed his farm in Texas, Hall looked up into its vortex. He described it as being hollow. The insides of it looked like a wobbly pipe that swayed in the wind. Hall said the vortex seemed to stretch 985 feet (300 meters) up and was 490 feet (150 meters) across.

Twister facts

The fastest winds on Earth blow inside tornadoes. Scientists think that they reach more than 300 miles (480 kilometers) per hour. They may be as fast as 500 miles (800 kilometers) per hour.

Multiple tornados

Some tornadoes break up into several mini tornadoes. The mini tornadoes are smaller than the tornado they come from, but they do just as much damage.

Two tornadoes have formed here. They are hitting the ground at the same time.

flash flood   flood that happens suddenly because of very heavy rain
severe   very bad or serious

Waterspouts

A tornado is a type of **whirlwind**. There are other types of whirlwinds, too. A **waterspout** is a spinning column of air above the sea or above a lake. Strong winds at the base of waterspouts make spray. This is sucked up into the spout.

Waterspout damage

When a waterspout dies out, the water in it drops back into the sea. Sometimes a waterspout moves over land before it dies out. Then, when it dumps its water, it can cause a **flash flood**.

△ These swirling ripples on the water's surface are caused by a waterspout. It has not picked up any water.

whirlwind spinning column of air

Dust devils

Another kind of whirlwind is a **dust devil.** Dust devils are also called land devils. A dust devil is a spinning column of air filled with dust, straw, and litter from the ground.

People often mistake dust devils for tornadoes because they look similar. A dust devil is very different from a tornado. It starts on the ground instead of in a cloud. Dust devils form in deserts and other hot, dry places. The Sun's rays heat the ground, and the ground heats the air above it. This hot air rises upward. If the wind swirls around a hillside, it can make the rising air spin. Dust devils can be more than 980 feet (300 meters) high.

◁ A giant waterspout, hundreds of feet high, is towering over the sea near Gerona, Spain.

Falling fish

A waterspout can suck up animals, such as small fish and crabs, from shallow water on the shore. If the spout moves over land and dies out, the animals are dropped onto the land in a shower!

The TORRO scale is a measure of tornado intensity used in the United Kingdom. It was made by the Tornado and Storm Research Organization in 1975. The TORRO scale goes from T1 to T10. T1 is a light tornado. This does little damage. T10 is a super tornado. The TORRO number and Fujita scale (opposite) are both based on the damage a tornado does.

Measuring tornadoes

Meteorologists measure the speed and direction of the wind, rainfall, **air pressure,** and temperature. They also measure tornadoes—but how? It is almost impossible to get inside a tornado to measure how fast the wind is blowing. The **intensity** of a tornado is measured by the damage it does. The damage gives an idea of the wind speeds inside.

A tornado caused millions of dollars worth of damage at this private airport in Texas.   ▽

air pressure   force of the air pressing down onto Earth
intensity   strength

The Fujita scale

The Fujita Tornado Scale grades the intensity of tornadoes in the United States. Professor Theodore Fujita invented the Fujita Tornado Scale at the University of Chicago in 1971. It measures the intensity of tornadoes on a scale of F0 to F5. F5 means the most **destruction.**

Mostly harmless

About two thirds of all tornadoes are weak. They last only a few minutes and normally do little damage. About a third of tornadoes are strong. They last twenty minutes or more. Only two percent of tornadoes are violent. They continue for more than an hour. They cause 70 percent of tornado deaths.

Professor Theodore Fujita and his tornado △ **simulator** at the University of Chicago in 1979.

Fujita scale	Wind speed	Type of damage
F0	40–72 miles (64–117 kilometers) per hour	Twigs and branches broken; small trees knocked over; some windows broken
F1	73–112 miles (118–180 kilometers) per hour	Roof tiles ripped off; mobile homes moved; cars slide off roads; large branches broken
F2	113–157 miles (181–251 kilometers) per hour	Whole roofs torn off; mobile homes smashed; some houses lifted off **foundations**; large trees fall; small objects fly through air
F3	158–206 miles (252–330 kilometers) per hour	Solid walls collapse; most trees uprooted; large cars thrown around; trains knocked over
F4	207–260 miles (331–417 kilometers) per hour	Houses completely destroyed; cars thrown and smashed; trees fly through air
F5	more than 261 miles (418 kilometers) per hour	Strong houses lifted and thrown around; cars fly through air; trains lifted off ground

meteorologist   scientist who studies the weather
simulator   equipment that copies a real event

Terrible Tornadoes

Most tornadoes do little damage. However, once in a while, a tornado causes a major disaster. Sometimes a single monster tornado, such as the Tri-State Tornado of 1925, does the damage. Occasionally it is a **swarm** of smaller tornadoes that cause terrible damage. This happened in Oklahoma in 1999.

May 4, 1999

Neighborhoods Wiped Out

Rescuers are searching through rubble for **victims** after dozens of tornadoes ripped through Oklahoma and Kansas yesterday. The twisters claimed 45 lives as thousands of homes were blown apart by winds of more than 300 miles (500 kilometers) per hour. "It looks like a bomb hit here," said a city official.

Houses in Oklahoma damaged and destroyed by a tornado from the 1999 tornado swarms. ▷

rubble   large pile of broken bits of things
suburb   area of houses on the edge of a city

A tornado swarm

On May 3, 1999, swarms of tornadoes touched down in Oklahoma and Kansas. The biggest swarm started in southwest Oklahoma and moved northeast to Oklahoma City. Some of the tornadoes were the biggest and most violent to strike Oklahoma ever. They were **intensity** F4 on the Fujita scale.

Disaster in Oklahoma City

One huge **twister** traveled for more than 40 miles (64 kilometers) until it hit the Oklahoma City **suburbs.** There, it flattened 1,000 homes. They were reduced to **rubble** and broken wood. Thousands of other homes were badly damaged. Sturdy factory buildings were ripped to shreds. Cars were thrown into the air.

Rescue difficulties

Rescuers in Oklahoma faced many problems. They tried to search for people in ruined homes, while even more tornadoes landed. Power lines were torn down and gas pipes were ripped apart. This caused blackouts and fires.

Violent tornado winds flipped this heavy truck on to its side. The truck was wrecked. ▽

Tri-State terror

The most deadly, single tornado on record hit the United States on March 18, 1925. It is known as the Tri-State Tornado. It left a wide strip of damage across the states of Missouri, Illinois, and Indiana. The tornado dropped from a huge thundercloud over southeast Missouri. It touched down near the town of Ellington. The Tri-State Tornado started small, but it grew quickly. It headed northeast. After tearing through Annapolis, it grew to 1 mile (1.6 kilometers) across and picked up speed. Traveling in a straight line at 60 miles (96 kilometers) per hour, the tornado flattened Gorham, Illinois. It sped on into Indiana, where it destroyed Griffin and much of Princeton.

" It made a **thundering roar** like a giant freight train. "

Survivor of the Tri-State Tornado, 1925

The Tri-State Tornado began in Missouri and left a trail of destruction across three states. ▽

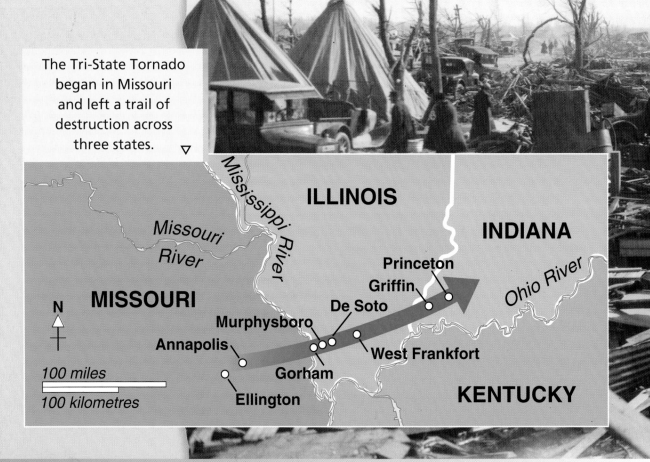

ILLINOIS

INDIANA

Mississippi River

Missouri River

Princeton
Griffin
De Soto

MISSOURI

N

Murphysboro

Ohio River

Annapolis

West Frankfort

100 miles
100 kilometres

Gorham

Ellington

KENTUCKY

destruction   being ruined or destroyed
victim   person injured or killed as a result of a bad event

A trail of destruction

Finally, the Tri-State Tornado died out. It had lasted an incredible three and a half hours. In that time, it covered 219 miles (353 kilometers). The path of **destruction** it left was 0.75 miles (1.2 kilometers) across. It wiped out four towns and badly damaged six more. The homes of 11,000 people were destroyed. Nearly 700 people died. Thousands more were injured. Worst hit was the town of Murphysboro, Illinois. Here, 234 people lost their lives. Most **victims** were taken by surprise because of the tornado's speed. At that time there were no warning systems.

Bangladesh tornado

The Tri-State Tornado was extremely damaging, but it did not cause the biggest tornado disaster ever. On April 2, 1977, a **swarm** of tornadoes hit Bangladesh. In the town of Madaripur, 900 people died and 6,000 were injured.

◁Homes in Indiana were reduced to **rubble** and trees were stripped of their branches by the Tri-State Tornado of 1925.

Where and When

Have you ever seen a real tornado? Your answer is probably no. Although tornadoes do not happen in many places, they do occur in more places than you might think. So where do they happen? What time of day and when in the year are they most common?

British tornadoes

Great Britain is not famous for its tornadoes, but many tornadoes and **waterspouts** touch down there every year. The southeast is most likely to be hit. Luckily, most are weak and last only a few minutes.

Tornado hot spots

The world's tornado **hot spot** is an area known as Tornado Alley in the United States. Three out of four of all tornadoes touch down in the United States.

◁ A mini tornado ripped out the wall of this house in Selsey, East Sussex, England, in 1998.

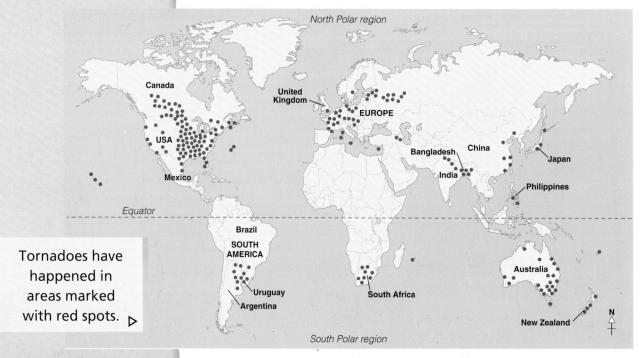

Tornadoes have happened in areas marked with red spots. ▷

front   place where warm air and cold air meet
midlatitudes   areas between Earth's polar regions and the tropics

Where fronts meet

Tornado hot spots are in areas of the world called the **midlatitudes**. They are between the **polar regions** and the **tropics**. In these places warm, moist air from the tropics meets cold, dry air from nearer the poles. The regions where the air masses meet are called **fronts**. Here, conditions are perfect to create the violent **supercell** thunderstorms. Tornadoes come from these.

A tornado is shown moving toward the yacht *Nicorette* during the Sydney to Hobart Yacht Race 2001. This is in the Bass Strait, between Australia and Tasmania. ▽

Australian tornadoes

Tornadoes are quite common in Australia. Most of them are very weak, but some are strong enough to damage property. Most Australian tornadoes are probably never reported because so few people live in the **outback**.

Twister facts

Between 800 and 1,200 tornadoes hit the United States every year. Of these tornadoes, about twenty measure F4 or F5 on the Fujita scale.

polar regions   areas at either end of Earth's axis
tropics   area of the world near the equator

Tornado times

In the places where tornadoes strike, there are more tornadoes at certain times of year. These are called tornado **seasons.** For example, the tornado season in the southeast United States is October and November. In Australia, the tornado season is November to May.

Tornadoes normally happen in the afternoon. Usually the sun has warmed the ground by then. The ground warms the air above it and clouds form. But tornadoes can land at any time of day, even at night. Night tornadoes are most dangerous, since it is difficult to see them coming.

Tornado times

An average tornado lasts for less than ten minutes and travels about 5 miles (8 kilometers). Some die away after a few seconds. Others last for more than an hour. Others hop along. They touch down for a few minutes and then lift up again.

Lightning streaks down from a huge thunderstorm at night. A deadly tornado under the storm would be ▽ difficult to see.

Twister facts

The average tornado speed is about 35 miles (55 kilometers) per hour. Some tornadoes do more than 60 miles (100 kilometers) per hour. That is as fast as a car on a highway.

hot spot   place where something happens often
season   period of the year with a special kind of weather

Tornado tracks

It is hard to **predict** where a tornado will go. Thunderstorms normally move steadily, but the tornado **vortex** sways around wildly. Some tornadoes move in huge circles as the storm moves along. A tornado can speed up, slow down, and swerve from side to side.

Ruined homes in Oklahoma in 1999. A few hundred feet away, homes were only slightly damaged. ▷

△ This tornado is in the far distance, but it could move in any direction. It could arrive here very soon.

23

Tornado Alley

One particular area of the world has more tornadoes than anywhere else. The area stretches through the center of the United States. It reaches from Texas in the south to North Dakota in the north. It is known as Tornado Alley. On some days, more than twenty tornadoes sweep through Tornado Alley.

Tornado Alley is the home of monster tornadoes. Right in the middle of Tornado Alley is Oklahoma. More tornadoes hit Oklahoma than any other state. The **peak** time for tornadoes here is May and June. At the southern end of Tornado Alley, peak times for tornadoes come earlier, between March and May.

Texas tornado

Texas is at the southern end of Tornado Alley. In May 1999 a **swarm** of eight tornadoes swept through central Texas. One giant tornado touched down for just five minutes. It flattened the small town of Jarrell, killing more than 30 people.

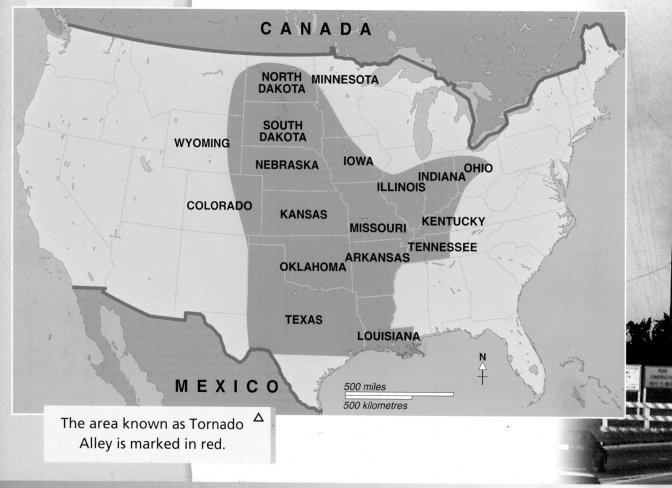

The area known as Tornado Alley is marked in red.

Storms on the plains

Why is Tornado Alley such a tornado **hot spot**? The answer is its position. Tornado Alley lies on huge, flat **plains** between the Gulf of Mexico and the Rocky Mountains. Warm, moist air comes from the Gulf of Mexico and cold, dry air flows from over the Rocky Mountains. The warm, moist air is near the ground and the cold, dry air is high in the **atmosphere.** These are perfect conditions for **supercell** thunderstorms to grow. Supercell thunderstorms create plenty of tornadoes.

One enormous tornado near the town of Jarrell, Texas, in Tornado Alley in 1997. The truck drivers are in great danger. ▽

A scene from the △ 1939 film *The Wizard of Oz,* showing the Scarecrow, Dorothy, and the Tin Man.

plains   very flat, wide areas of the countryside
supercell   extremely violent thunderstorm

Signs and Warnings

What is it like to be in the path of a huge tornado? What would you do to protect yourself from these monsters? What happens to buildings when a tornado sweeps through? How do you return to normal? Let us examine the journey of a tornado from start to finish.

Green clouds

Thunderclouds can look slightly green. This is often a sign of heavy **hail** inside the cloud. Heavy hail shows that a thunderstorm is very violent. It may turn into a tornado.

△ Giant hail stones like these can damage property and injure people and animals when they fall.

This mammatus cloud △ is a sure sign that a tornado is about to form.

hail   balls of ice and tightly packed snow
mammatus cloud   hanging loops of cloud

Gathering clouds

People who live in Tornado Alley know when tornadoes are likely to form. The first sign is thunderclouds building in the distance. These can be spotted by their anvil tops. From a distance, the clouds bulge out on top. This shows that the **updrafts** in the cloud are very strong. So the storm may be a powerful **supercell**.

More signs

The thunderstorm gets closer. The sky is full of dark clouds. Lumps of clouds hang down from underneath. These kinds of cloud are called **mammatus clouds.** They show that the tops of the thunderclouds have moved downward. The storm is at its strongest, and a tornado is likely to form soon.

Then, the bottom of the thundercloud drops down toward the ground. It makes a circular wall of cloud several miles across. The wall slowly spins around. This cloud is called a wall cloud. A wall cloud is seen just before many tornadoes touch down.

Clear blue skies

Sunshine does not make you safe from a tornado. A tornado sometimes comes down from the edge of a thunderstorm. It can touch the ground where the sun is shining.

Sun shining on a tornado. This shows that good weather can be very close to a ▽ violent tornado.

Watches and warnings

Weather **forecasters** are always checking for **supercell** thunderstorms. They issue a warning called a tornado watch. This does not mean tornadoes are definitely going to come, but rather that people should be alert over the next day or so. They should listen to the radio and watch television for more information. In areas where tornadoes are common, people have special weather radios. These are just for receiving tornado news.

Then a tornado warning is **broadcast** on radio and television. A tornado is likely to touch down very soon or one has already been seen. The local tornado warning **siren** is set off.

Subject: Tornado Watch
Time: 4:30 P.M. Monday, May 3, 1999

The Storm Prediction Center has issued a tornado watch for western and central Oklahoma. Tornadoes, **hail,** thunderstorm wind gusts to 80 miles (130 kilometers) per hour, and dangerous lightning are possible in this area. Be on the lookout for threatening weather conditions. Listen for later statements and possible warnings.

Where not to hide

Some people believe that it is safe to swim across a river to escape from a tornado. But tornadoes can cross very wide rivers. Hills and mountains are not safe, either. Tornadoes have swept over the tops of mountains.

△ This tornado is sweeping over mountains in Montana.

broadcast   send information over the radio or television
forecaster   person who figures out what the weather will be like in the future

Finding shelter

People should find shelter as soon as possible. This is very important in heavy rain or at night, because the tornado could arrive by surprise. Most schools, offices, and factories have strong tornado shelters. At home, people should go into their bathrooms or **basements**. A bathroom is normally the strongest room in a house. People in the outdoors should lie down in ditches or under strong road bridges.

Safe rooms

A few homes have tornado-safe rooms. A safe room is a very strong room designed to stand up to the fiercest tornadoes. It is made from steel or **reinforced** concrete. Safe rooms are often built in the center of houses.

◁ An underground tornado shelter in Oklahoma. The heavy concrete roof protects people from the violent winds.

reinforced   made stronger
siren   machine that makes a very loud warning noise

A Tornado Strikes

People hide in their shelters. There are loud claps of thunder outside. Lightning streaks across the dark sky. Heavy rain floods the ground. Giant **hail** stones crash down. A **funnel** cloud drops from the wall cloud under the thunderstorm. The funnel quickly gets longer until it hits the ground. The tornado has touched down!

The tornado begins to suck up dust as soon as it hits the ground. Its **vortex** turns black. Warm air from near the ground feeds the tornado. It grows until it is 1,312 feet (400 meters) across. It moves across the fields at 40 miles (64 kilometers) per hour.

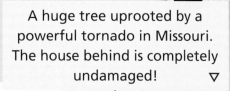

A huge tree uprooted by a powerful tornado in Missouri. The house behind is completely undamaged! ▽

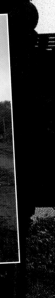

Debris is hurled around. A tornado △ sweeps through the streets of Salt Lake City, Utah, in 1999.

crop   plant that can be grown and sold

Tornado damage

Tornadoes do so much damage because of their incredible winds. They blow around the vortex and also swirl upward. They push, pull, and twist objects. Things are moved, lifted, bent, and broken by the winds.

Destruction begins

The tornado rips **crops** from the fields. It moves on to the woods. Its winds pull some trees from the ground. Other trees are twisted and their trunks split apart. The tornado crosses a road. It tears open the road surface. It snaps a line of thick telephone poles. Drivers leave their cars and take cover in ditches. Their vehicles are sucked up and hurled aside. They are destroyed. Trucks are knocked off the road.

Dangerous cars

Cars are not safe places to be during tornadoes. In 1989 a tornado struck in Huntsville, Alabama. Twenty-one people were killed. Twelve of them were seeking shelter in their cars.

△ The remains of a car wrecked and wrapped around a tree by a tornado.

Tornado in town

Now the tornado arrives at the edge of town. **Storm spotters** are outside, **tracking** its movements. They have radioed ahead to warn people it is on the way. People are sitting in their tornado shelters, their bathrooms, safe rooms, and **basements**. If they are lucky, the tornado will miss their homes. Screaming and roaring noises come from close by. It is terrifying. Then the tornado arrives. Some people are not lucky, and their houses are destroyed.

Trailer parks

Mobile homes are often the worst places to be in a tornado. They are very light and very weak. The homes have no **foundations** under the ground, as a house does, and are easily blown away— even if they are tied down.

Survivors of the Oklahoma City tornado of 1999 are searching through their home. It has been blown apart. ▽

△ A mobile home is sometimes one of the worst places to be in a tornado. This one was flipped over by a mini tornado in France.

foundation heavy base on which a building stands
storm spotter person who watches out for tornadoes and warns people

Flattened homes

Our houses and apartments seem like strong and safe places to be, but they are toys to a tornado! How does this happen?

When a tornado's winds hit a house, they blow over it and around its sides. The fast moving air rushes past and sucks the roof upward. With winds of 200 miles (320 kilometers) per hour, this suction is huge and lifts the roof off. This weakens the structure of the house. Then, the wall facing the wind blows in.

Keep them closed

Many years ago people were advised to open their windows during a tornado to let air out. This is not a good idea. Flying glass is more likely to hit people.

A tornado ripped apart the strong steel frame of this factory building in Douglasville, Georgia.
▽

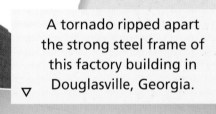

Flying debris

The tornado's fierce winds are dangerous to people who are outside. The winds pick up objects from destroyed houses, streets, and gardens. These flying objects, called **debris,** are more dangerous than the winds themselves. The winds of a tornado spiral inward and upward at great speed. Objects are dragged up into the **vortex** and fly around in it. Things are thrown toward the outside, like clothes in a clothes dryer. They are flung out of the sides of the vortex, often for hundreds of feet.

A steel kitchen sink wrapped around a tree branch by an F5 tornado that hit Oklahoma City in 1999. ▽

Strange events

Tornadoes have been known to carry things a very long way. In 1979 bank checks plucked by a tornado from a bank in Oklahoma landed more than 480 mi (300 km) away in Texas.

The twisted metal in this tree is the remains of a road sign ◁ thrown through the air.

Deadly straws

Even the smallest objects become deadly in a tornado. A tornado can pick up a piece of straw from a field and blow it at solid wood. The end of the straw can sink into the wood like a dart, because it goes so fast.

Twister facts

In 1973 a tornado hit Nebraska. Many houses were destroyed. The tornado sucked a grand piano from one of them. It weighed 507 lb (230 kg). It was found 1,312 ft (400 m) away.

Deadly missiles

A powerful tornado can pick up very big and heavy objects, including cars, trucks, train cars, and even whole houses. Objects turn into deadly **missiles** because of the wind's speed. Bits of houses, fences, street signs, and branches all whiz through the air. They do incredible damage to anything they hit. Even tiny things can be **lethal** missiles at 200 mi (320 km) per hour. Flying glass is especially dangerous.

missile weapon that flies through the air

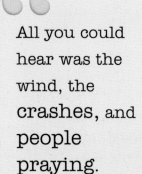

A scene of destruction

The terrible roaring noise dies away. The tornado leaves as quickly as it arrived. People come out of their shelters. It is quiet and the sun is shining. However, some people are unlucky. Where their homes once stood there are piles of twisted **debris.** Parts of houses are mixed with broken furniture, smashed televisions, refrigerators, and other precious possessions. Their cars have completely disappeared. These people have nothing left. They are lucky to be alive.

A narrow strip

The tornado has cut a narrow strip through the town. Inside the strip, everything is destroyed, but a few feet away, on either side, there is no damage at all. Damage from tornadoes is always like this. It is very **localized.** A tornado can wipe away one house, but leave the house next door untouched.

△ Firefighters clearing up debris after a mini tornado struck a house in northern France. They are also making sure there are no loose roof tiles left to fall.

downdraft   current of air that flows downward
localized   just in one small area

Clearing up

Police, paramedics, and firefighters arrive on the scene. They rush injured **victims** to the hospital. Then they search through the **rubble** for missing people. Shelters with food and beds are set up. Homeless people rest here until they find places to stay with family and friends. After a violent, giant tornado, a **national emergency** may be declared. The army could be called in to help rescue people and clean up. People may be given money to help rebuild their homes.

Dying away

Many miles away, the tornado is finally dying out. **Downdrafts** of cold air from high up have cut off its supply of warm air. It runs out of energy. Its **vortex** takes the shape of a long, writhing snake. It fades. Then it is gone.

A small risk

Even in Tornado Alley, the chances of being hit by a tornado in a lifetime are very small. Still, some unlucky people have been hit twice. A few have been hit three times!

△ A victim is rushed into an ambulance after being injured when a large exhibition tent collapsed in a tornado in Salt Lake City, Utah.

△ Home owners in Ohio are shown here after a tornado destroyed their homes.

national emergency   disaster so large that a country's armed forces are sent to help; government money is used to help people

Fighting Tornadoes

TOTO

Project TOTO was an early attempt at tornado research in the 1980s. TOTO stands for Totable Tornado Observatory. It was named after Toto, the dog in *The Wizard of Oz.* Researchers were supposed to drop this **device** into a tornado from the back of a truck. Sadly, it was never successful.

Tornadoes are very powerful. There is nothing we can do to stop them. In the United States, people are killed by tornadoes every year. Hundreds are injured. Millions of dollars worth of damage is done to homes and businesses. It is very important for us to try to understand tornadoes. Then we can attempt to **predict** them and warn people.

Tornado research

Weather experts still have a lot to learn about tornadoes. They have one big problem. There is very little information about what happens inside tornadoes, and it would be crazy to go into a tornado to find out!

A tornado researcher inside the Doppler on Wheels. ▽

△ This truck is called a Doppler on Wheels. **Doppler radar** is the type of radar found mounted on the back of a truck. It measures wind speeds inside the tornado.

analyze   look at very carefully
device   small machine

Project VORTEX

Project VORTEX is the biggest **research** project so far into tornadoes. In 1995 scientists from the National **Severe** Storm Laboratory photographed tornadoes. They also used **radar** to measure the wind speeds inside them. The information from Project VORTEX is still being **analyzed**.

Future measurement

Researchers need detailed information from the insides of tornadoes and **supercell** thunderstorms. To get this information, scientists are developing new instruments and machines. New radars will be able to look into tornadoes and accurately measure winds. Researchers are also developing machines called turtles. These are small, tough, remote-control tanks. They will be able to carry measuring instruments into the path of a tornado without being damaged.

Hard to find

A big problem for tornado researchers is finding a tornado to research! There are only three a day in the entire United States. Professor Fujita, who created the Fujita scale, had to wait 30 years to see a tornado!

Meteorologists prepare to launch a weather balloon into a storm. Instruments carried by the balloon measure the temperature and **air pressure** of the supercell thunderstorm.

radar   machine that uses radio waves to detect objects in the distance
research   collecting and studying information about something

Tornado watching

Tornadoes are complicated things. **Meteorologists** cannot **predict** if tornadoes will definitely happen in a certain place. Before a tornado forms, there are often certain types of weather. Meteorologists can recognize these signs and warn people if tornadoes are likely in their area.

Weather **forecasters** gather information from **satellites,** weather balloons, and weather stations. They put this information into computers. Computer programs figure out what the weather may be like over the next few hours and days. The computers may predict **severe** thunderstorms. Forecasters can then tell people to expect tornadoes.

Hook trace

A Doppler radar screen shows bright colors where the strongest winds are in a thunderstorm. A spinning column of air inside a thunderstorm always shows up on the screen as a bright hook shape. If there is a hook shape, a tornado is most probably on its way.

△ A Doppler radar screen showing severe thunderstorms at the top. Tornadoes could be forming in the yellow patches.

△ Meteorologists follow the progress of thunderstorms in Tornado Alley. The information they are examining comes from radars, satellites, and weather stations.

Doppler radar   radar that can measure the speed of air inside clouds
predict   say what will happen in the future

Storm spotters

If thunderstorms do begin to form, then forecasters in the local area begin to work hard. They use special **radars** called **Doppler radars.** These radars detect moving air. They measure the speeds of winds inside severe thunderstorms. If forecasters see a spinning column of air on their radar screens, they put out a warning to say tornadoes are likely soon.

Local people called **storm spotters** go out in their cars to search for tornadoes and track them. They report their sightings to the local tornado warning center. People in the path of a storm can be warned to take shelter. Storm spotting is a dangerous job. All storm spotters are specially trained in safety.

Storm chasers

Storm chasers are different than storm spotters. They are people interested in tornadoes who chase severe thunderstorms in their cars. They hope to see tornadoes and photograph or video them. Storm chasing is a dangerous hobby.

Storm chasers photographing lightning from a huge thunderstorm.

Be prepared

Your chances of surviving a tornado are quite high. In fact, 99 percent of people live to tell the tale. Your chances are better if you have a place to take shelter and an emergency plan. You should have a tornado drill like the one on the next page. You must practice your drill, so you remember what to do if the real thing happens. Every second counts when a tornado is on the way. You should put together an emergency kit. It should include a radio (with spare batteries), a flashlight, a first-aid kit, and a map. You can then follow the progress of a tornado.

Twister facts

In June 1990 a tornado touched down in Indiana. It was heading toward the Bolding family's home. They took shelter in their downstairs bathroom, but Ross, who was eight years old, was missing. The tornado struck and destroyed the house. Afterward the worried family found Ross 328 feet (100 meters) away. Apart from some bruises, he was fine. He could not remember a thing!

When you see a sky like this, a tornado could be on its way. ▽

A child's bicycle was wrapped around a tree ◁ by a F4 tornado.

TORNADO DRILL

- Listen to the radio or watch the television for tornado warnings
- Go quickly to your tornado shelter, safe room, or **basement**
- Stay away from windows at all times
- If a tornado hits, kneel down with your hands over your head
- Beware of flying **debris**
- Do not leave your shelter until the all-clear is given
- If you are in a car or bus, get out. Lie face down in a ditch with your hands over your head

Safer and safer

Because of better **forecasting** and warnings, the number of people killed by tornadoes is going down. In the U.S., about 80 people die per year, while in the 1930s it was 200 a year.

Even though tornadoes do terrible damage, you are unlikely to get caught in one. ◁

Find Out More

Organizations

The National Weather Service

An organization that keeps track of weather conditions around the country. The National Weather Service occasionally issues severe weather warnings when necessary. Contact them at the following address: **National Weather Service, National Oceanic and Atmospheric Administration, US Dept. of Commerce, 1325 East West Highway, Silver Spring, MD 20910 www.nws.noaa.gov**

Books

Chambers, Catherine. *Disasters in Nature: Tornadoes.* Chicago: Heinemann Library, 2000.

O'Neill Grace, Catherine. *Forces of Nature.* Washington, D.C.: National Geographic Society, 2004.

Steele, Christy. *Nature on the Rampage: Tornadoes.* Chicago: Raintree, 2004.

World Wide Web

If you want to find out more about tornadoes, you can search the Internet using keywords such as these:

- tornado + news
- wind + disasters
- tornado + safety

You can also find your own keywords by using headings or words from this book. Use the search tips on the next page to help you find the most useful websites.

Search tips

There are billions of pages on the Internet, so it can be difficult to find exactly what you want to find. For example, if you just type in "tornado" on a search engine such as Google, you'll get a list of millions of web pages. These tips will help you find useful websites more quickly:

- Decide exactly what you want to find out about first.
- Use simple keywords instead of whole sentences.
- Use two to six keywords in a search, putting the most important words first.
- Be precise—use names of people, places, or things when you can.
- If your keywords are made up of two or more words that go together, put quote marks around them—for example, "Fujita scale."
- Use the "+" sign to join keywords together—for example, "weather + disaster."

Where to search

Search engine

A search engine looks through millions of web pages and lists all the sites that match the words in the search box. They can give thousands of links, but the best matches are at the top of the list, on the first page. Try **google.com**.

Search directory

A search directory is more like a library of websites that have been sorted by a person instead of a computer. You can search by keyword or subject and browse through the different sites in the same way you would look through books on a library shelf. A good example is **yahooligans.com**.

45

Glossary

air pressure   force of the air pressing down onto Earth

analyze   look at very carefully

atmosphere   layer of air around Earth

basement   room in the ground under a house

broadcast   send information over the radio or television

chaos   total confusion

condense   when a gas turns into a liquid

crop   plant that can be grown and sold

cumulonimbus   very tall, large cloud

current   flow of air or water

debris   bits and pieces of wrecked houses, cars, and other objects

destruction   being ruined or destroyed

device   small machine

Doppler radar   radar that can measure the speed of air moving inside clouds

downdraft   current of air that flows downward

dust devil   spinning column of air filled with dust, straw, and trash

evidence   proof that something has happened

eyewitness   someone who saw something happen

flash flood   flood that happens suddenly because of very heavy rain

forecaster   person who figures out what the weather will be like in the future

foundation   heavy base on which a building stands

front   place where warm air and cold air meet

funnel   shape that is like a cone with a long, thin section coming from the smaller, bottom end

hail   balls of ice and tightly packed snow

hot spot   place where something happens often

intensity   strength

lethal   able to cause death

localized   just in one small area

mammatus cloud   hanging loops of cloud

meteorologist   scientist who studies the weather

midlatitudes   areas between Earth's polar regions and the tropics

missile   weapon that flies through the air

national emergency   disaster so large that a country's armed forces are sent to help; government money is used to help people

outback   out of the way, inland areas of Australia

peak   highest point or greatest amount

plains   very flat, wide areas of the countryside

polar regions areas at either end of Earth's axis. Earth's axis is an imaginary line that runs through the center of Earth, about which the planet rotates.

predict say what will happen in the future

radar machine that uses radio waves to detect objects in the distance

random happens without any pattern or choice

reinforced made stronger

research collecting and studying information about something

rubble large pile of broken bits of things

satellite object that moves around Earth in space

season period of the year with a special kind of weather

severe very bad or serious

simulator equipment that copies a real event

siren machine that makes a very loud warning noise

storm spotter person who watches out for tornadoes and warns people

suburb area of houses on the edge of a city

supercell extremely violent thunderstorm

swarm large group of things moving close together

torrential like a torrent, which is a rushing stream of liquid

track look for signs and follow

tropics area of the world near the equator. The equator is an imaginary line that runs around the center of Earth at a equal distance from both the north and south poles.

twister common name for a tornado

updraft current of air that flows upward

victim person injured or killed as a result of a bad event

vortex scientific name for a spinning column of air

waterspout spinning column of air above a sea or lake

water vapor water in the form of an invisible gas

whirlwind spinning column of air

Index